GOD'S LOVE

INRODUCTION

I am a child of God; this is the word of God. I am what the word of God says that I am; I can do what the word of God says I can do; I can have what the word of God says I can have. I am the righteousness of God. Therefore, I walk by faith and not by sight. I am above and not beneath. I am the head and not the tail. Faith cometh by hearing and hearing by the word of God and having heard the word of God, I have applied the word to my life, to expect the manifestation of the father's promises to be fulfilled in my life. To Jesus be all the praise, honor and glory both now and forever. Amen (so be it).

In today's world of terror and hatred, knowing God's love is of the utmost importance. We must know and testify that Heavenly Father and Jesus the Messiah are glorified, living, loving beings. "For God so loved the world that he gave his only Son, that whoever believes in him should not perish but have eternal life." Jesus "so loved the world that he gave his own life that whoever believes become the sons of God." Yes, the Father and the Son are one—in purpose and in love.

MY IMAGE OF GOD AND I

How I imagine God is directly related to myself: My image of God influences my thinking and my actions. If God is far away and I don't think he's listening to me, then I don't need to look to him for help. If God is a strict father, there may come a time when I don't want to have anything to do with him anymore. Because God then brings more bad than good into my life: fear and pressure to perform.

But how do you know which idea of God is correct? And doesn't the Bible itself say that I shouldn't have a rigid image of him? (Exodus 20:4) Isn't my idea of God always human and flawed? Also, as a human being, I cannot define what God is like, because I can never fully understand God. I only know what is in the sky, on the earth, and in the sea. But he stands outside of it.

It becomes clear: If I want to form an image of God for myself, it must be given to me. God hath to show me himself what he is like. And that's what he does according to Christian understanding. Accordingly, the Bible shows how God was experienced and experienced and what he said about himself. This image of God is to be presented in the following to some extent.

GOD SHOWS HIMSELF AS LOVE.

According to the Bible, God is a spirit who is eternal, invisible, and unchanging. And at the same time, omniscient and omnipotent. The whole world came into being through him alone. He alone is the source of all life (Hebrews 11:3). As the creator, God does not have to justify his actions to anyone (Isaiah 40:13-15). One reason is that we, as creatures, cannot always understand his actions with our limited vision. As God says in the Bible, "My thoughts are not your thoughts, and my ways are not your ways. For as the heavens are higher than the earth, so are my ways higher than your ways, and my thoughts than your thoughts" (Isaiah 55:8-9). This means that even if we cannot always understand God, we can trust him.

Elsewhere, Jesus emphasizes that we can trust God because God takes care of even the details of our life. The train of thought: God already endows the flowers with great beauty. And he takes care of small, insignificant sparrows. However, because man is more valuable than flowers and sparrows, he can be sure that God will take care of him (Matthew 6:25-34). So I don't have to worry because I can trust God.

GOD SHOWS HIMSELF AS SAVIOR.

Concretely, God proves through his actions that he means business when he offers to help people. The person who relies on God can count on God's help and experience it. God cares about people and their needs. He wants to be there to help people. So it was recorded in the Bible: All who entrust themselves to you [God] will shout for joy! Those who know and love you as Savior will always cry out: "Great is the Lord!" (Psalms 40:17).

With God, man experiences salvation and care. He can give a man what he needs because he is almighty and knows his creatures inside and out (Matthew 10:30). There is also no limit or limitation to God's help. He can come to God with everything that weighs on man: injustice, worries, fears, his own failure and guilt, questions about the meaning of life, illness, depression, etc. God does not promise to fulfill all of man's wishes, but he promises to fulfill his to help and take care of problems.

God also points out that it is futile for people to put all their hope in things that perish or in other people: "I want you to know me and trust me. You should understand: I am the only God. There is no God who came before me, and there will never be another. I, the Lord, am the only God. Only I can save you. I have let you know and have always helped you. You heard about me through the prophets. Have you ever known another god with such power? You are witnesses that I alone am God" (Isaiah 43:10-12).

GOD SHOWS HIMSELF AS A JUDGE.

But God doesn't just do something good for people by helping them with problems. He also gives him orientation and rules. In our world, it becomes clear that just and wise laws are of great help:

Every society has certain moral guidelines. Without laws and courts that make binding rules for a society, the law of the strongest quickly prevails. The weaker one is then no longer worth much and is helplessly at the mercy of corruption and injustice. God's laws also have this purpose. What human governments are supposed to do on a small scale in our world, God does as a judge on a even larger scale.

God is described in the Bible as morally perfectly good: "All that God gives us is good and perfect. He, the Father of Light, does not change; light and darkness never change in him." (James 1:17) Because God is perfectly good and never changes, he can also set the standard for what is good for us humans and what righteous behavior means. God's laws can be summarized as follows: "The Lord has long since told you what is good! He asks only one thing of you: do what is right, treat others with kindness, and live in reverence for your God!" (Micah 6:8). One day God will therefore also judge this world and all people justly and enforce his perfect justice. In a letter from the New Testament, the author Peter confesses: "But we are all waiting for the new heavens and the new earth, which God has promised us. We are waiting for this new world in which there will finally be justice" (2 Peter 3:13).

GOD SHOWS HIMSELF AS FATHER.

In the image of the father, God's view of people becomes even clearer: According to the Bible, he wants to accompany us like a father throughout life. Humans long for affection and security, which is particularly evident in childhood. But even as an adult, this longing has not disappeared. God wants to be that person and satisfy that longing. With him, one is never alone but can experience security. This is what God says in the Bible to the Israelites, to whom he had revealed himself in a special way: "Listen to me, you descendants of Jacob, all of you who are left of Israel! I have carried you from the beginning; I have taken care of you since you were born. I stay the same; I will carry you to old age until you turn gray. I, the Lord, have done it hitherto, and I will carry you and save you in the future" (Isaiah 46:3-4).

God wants to live in a very personal relationship with his creatures. Just as a good father cares for, guides, and protects his children, God desires that relationship with a man. At the same time, however, God gives people the freedom to live in this father-child relationship or not. He does not restrict people in his love.

In the well-known parable of the prodigal son (Luke 15), this attitude of God is particularly well illustrated: The father (God) possesses all the fullness that he generously gives to his son (man). But the son wants nothing more to do with him. He would rather discover what the world has to offer outside of his homeland and his father's court. The father gives him this freedom but is very happy to take his son back when he later returns to him because he realizes that things are worse for him abroad than at home. God's fatherly love is also shown by the fact that he is merciful and willingly forgives guilt when a person admits his guilt and turns to God.

GOD SHOWS HIMSELF AS LOVE.

It even becomes clear in the Bible that God not only loves man but that he is love. God's actions and being are completely permeated with love. With God, there is no contradiction between what he is and what he does. Everything God does is done out of love because God is love.

We do not need to demand love from God. We don't have to work hard to earn it either. He gives it to us voluntarily always. All people, a person's actions may affect his relationship with God; for example, God's love may not penetrate the person. Yet God's love for man is always the same because it is unconditional.

This love of God is most evident in the fact that God gave everything that man had for the man. The Bible says: "Love comes from God [...] because God is love. God's love for us became visible to all when he sent his only son into the world so that we might live through him. What is unique about this love is that we did not love God, but he gave us his love" (1 John 4:7-10). God not only says that he loves a man with all his heart, but he proves it by giving man the most precious thing he has: his son Jesus Christ.

In Jesus, God also shows his nature as a father in a special way. For Jesus testified to his followers: "Whoever has seen me has also seen the Father. [...] Don't you think that I am in the Father, and the Father is in me? I didn't makeup what I'm telling you myself. My Father, who lives in me, acts through me. Believe me that the Father and I are one" (John 14:9-11). Jesus Christ is a perfect reflection of God because he lives in full trust and fellowship with

God. In the gospels, you can still read how Jesus lived and thus understand what God really is like. For "Christ is the image of the invisible God" (Colossians 1:15).

THE LOVE OF GOD IS PERFECT AND LIMITLESS.

The love of God is divine by definition. The scriptures also declare it to be perfect or finished. It is limitless because the atonement is a sacrifice of love for all who have lived, who are living now, and who will live in the future. It is also limitless because time has no limits to it.

THE LOVE OF GOD IS CONSTANT.

The love of God is constant. "Even after a thousand generations, he keeps the covenant and shows his kindness to those who love him and keep his commands."

THE LOVE OF GOD IS ALL-ENCOMPASSING.

The love of God is all-encompassing. God "makes his sun rise on the evil and on the good, and sends rain on the just and on the unjust." Jesus is the light of the world, who gives life to everything and is the law. "He invites… all to come to him; …and he refuses no one who comes to him—black or white, bond or free, male or female." All are invited to pray to Heavenly Father.

THE LOVE OF GOD IS NOT UNCONDITIONAL.

While the love of God is perfect, infinite, enduring, and universal, it would be wrong to say that it is unconditional. This is not said in the scriptures. On the other hand, many verses affirm that the higher level of love shown by the Father and the Son, and certain blessings that flow from that love, are conditional. Before giving examples of this, let us consider the various expressions for such conditions found in the scriptures.

DIFFERENT EXPRESSIONS FOR THE CONDITIONS

Various expressions for the conditions are found in the scriptures:

"If... [Certain conditions are met], then... [Certain consequences occur]." (If and then are either stated explicitly or implied.)

"If ... [certain conditions are met] ... [certain consequences occur]."

"If... not... can't... not. ... "

For example, in verse dealing with our creation, the most important reason why we are on earth is stated: "We want to test them through this and see if they will do all that also always the Lord their God commands them." Life here is a probationary period. Our thoughts and actions determine whether we will prove ourselves in mortality and thus be accepted in heaven.

GOD'S LOVE IS CONDITIONAL.

As we consider the various forms of condition found in the scriptures, many verses draw our attention to the conditional nature of God's love for us. Examples of this:

"If you keep my commands, [then] you will remain in my love, just as I have kept my Father's commands and remain in his love.

"If ye do not keep my commands, [then] the love of the Father shall not dwell upon you."

"If anyone loves me, [then] he will keep my word: my father will love him."

"I love all who love me, and whoever seeks me will find me."

"Now I understand that God does not look to persons, but welcomes in every nation those who fear him and do what is right."

The Lord "loves those who would have him for their God."

"Whoever has my commands and keeps them, it is he who loves me; but whoever loves me will be loved by my Father, and I also will love him and will reveal myself to him."

GOD'S BLESSINGS ARE CONDITIONAL.

It is equally evident that the loving Lord bestows upon us certain blessings only when the specified conditions are met. Examples of this:

"If you walk in my ways, obey my laws and commands... then I will give you a long life."

"If you obey my commands and keep my statutes and do and obey all my commands... then I will make the word true on you."

"I, the Lord, am bound if ye do as I say; but if you do not what I say, you have no promise."

"If we obtain any blessing from God, it is only by obedience to the law on which it is based."

"A law is given to every kingdom, and to every law, there are also certain limits and conditions."

The Lord has said: "All who desire a blessing from me must keep the law appointed for that blessing and its conditions, which were established before the foundation of the world. ...

And now as to the new and everlasting covenant, it was established for the fullness of my glory; and whoever receives an abundance of it must and will keep the law, lest he is damned, saith the Lord God.

The terms of this law are: All covenants, contracts, obligations, commitments, oaths, vows, actions, bonds, agreements, and expectations not made and entered into and sealed both for time and for all eternity - by the who anointed have no efficacy, power, or validity at the resurrection from the dead and after."

There are other laws designed to bless us here on earth. This includes the law of tithing. "Bring all the tithes to the storehouse. . . . Test me with it, says the Lord; those who do not pay to tithe have no promise.

Again, "All he asks of you is that you keep his commands; and he promised you that if ye keep his commands, ye shall prosper in the land; and he never deviates from what he has spoken; therefore, if you keep his commands, he will bless you and prosper you."

Why is God's love conditional? Because God loves us and wants us to be happy. "Happiness is the purpose and purpose of our existence and that goal will be attained if we follow the path that leads to it. That path is called virtue, blamelessness, faithfulness, and obedience to all the commandments of God."

HOW CAN WE PROTECT OURSELVES FROM FALSE IDEAS?

When we understand that God's love and blessings do not come "unconditionally," we can avoid being lured into popular heresies such as, "Because God loves everyone unconditionally, he loves me even then." if I…" or "Because God is love, he loves me unconditionally, without looking at it…."

Such arguments are used by opponents of Christ to deceive people with flattery. Nehor, for example, put himself in the limelight by preaching false teachings. He "also tested to the people that all men would be saved at the last day...for the Lord created all men...and in the end, all men would have eternal life." Unfortunately, some people believed Nehor's fallacious teachings of God's unconditional love.

Contrary to what Nehor taught, the love of God reminds us, "Being wicked never brought happiness." Jesus declares, "Come unto me and be saved. . . . If you do not keep my commands . . . you will by no means enter the kingdom of heaven."

THE LOVE OF GOD AND SINNERS

Does this mean that the Lord does not love the sinner? Of course not. The love of God is infinite and all-encompassing. The Savior loves both the saint and the sinner. The apostle John confirms this: "We will love because he first loved us." 39 And Nephi, who had seen in a vision the mortal work of the Lord, wrote: "And because of their iniquity the world will judge him, he be nothing; wherefore they scourge him, and he endures it; they beat him, and he endures it; yea, they spit on him, and he endures it with loving kindness, and for long-suffering toward the sons of men." We know how far-reaching the Redeemer's love is, for he died so that all could who die can come to life again.

IMMORTALITY AND ETERNAL LIFE

God has said that His eternal work and glory is "to bring to pass the immortality and life of man." Because of the atonement, we receive the gift of immortality without conditions. However, the greater gift of eternal life is conditional. To qualify for it is to abstain from all that is ungodly, and to honor the ordinances and covenants of the temple. The rich bouquet of God's love—which includes eternal life—includes blessings to which we must make ourselves worthy and are not entitled if we are unworthy. The sinner cannot submit the Lord's will to his own and ask Him to be blessed in his sins. Whoever wants to enjoy every single flower in the magnificent bouquet must practice repentance.

CALL TO REPENTANCE

"Every blessing the Lord bestows on His people is conditional. These conditions are: 'Obey my law, keep my commands, walk in my ordinances, and keep my statutes, love my mercies...keep thyself pure in the law, and then thou art entitled to these blessings, but not before."

"Thus I see the conditions that God has set for His people as a body and for each individual, and I believe that I thank God or my brethren are not entitled to blessings, favors, trust, and love from them until I have proven by my works that I am worthy of them. I never expect to receive blessings I do not deserve."

Given that we are all imperfect, it is important that each individual takes responsibility for their life. Those who repent and keep the Lord's commands will find forgiveness.

"And whoever does not repent, even the light that he received will be taken away from him; for my spirit will not always labor or stride with man, saith the Lord."

In repentance, both the effort and the result count. The Lord has said that spiritual gifts come to those "who love me and keep all my commands, and... seek to do these things."

THE LOVE OF GOD SHOWS US THE WAY.

Jesus asked us to love one another as he loved us. Is that even possible? Can the love we feel for other people really match the love of God? Yes, she can! The pure love of Christ comes to all who seek and qualify for it. Such love also includes the willingness to serve and obey.

Obeying the law of God requires faith. This is the linchpin of the trials we face here on earth. At the same time, through our faith, we demonstrate our love for God. The more determined we are to pattern our lives after His example, the purer and more divine our love will become.

There is probably no love here on earth that comes closest to the love of God than the love that parents have for their children. For we as parents have the same responsibility to teach our children obedience as our Heavenly Parent does when He felt to command to teach us. While we can make it clear that we must tolerate those who are different from us, we must not tolerate our children breaking the laws of God. They must learn the doctrines of the kingdom, trust in the Lord, and know that blessings will come to them only if they first keep His commands.

The love of God is perfect, infinite, constant, and all-encompassing. The full measure of that love and the greatest blessings it brings are conditional—they require our obedience to the eternal law. It is my prayer that we may qualify and enjoy these blessings forever.

Why is God's love conditional? Because God loves us and wants us to be happy. "Happiness is the purpose and purpose of our existence and that goal will be attained if we follow the path that leads to it.

What is true love that touches every heart? Why does the simple statement "I love you" bring joy to everyone?

People give various reasons for this. The real reason, however, is that every person who comes to earth is a spirit, son, or daughter of God. All love emanates from God, and therefore we are born with the ability and desire to love and be loved. One of the strongest connections we retain to the premortal life is a sense of how much The Heavenly Father and Jesus loved us and how much we loved them. A veil has been placed over our memories, but whenever we feel true love, there is undeniably a yearning.

It is part of our being that we respond to true love. We have an innate desire to feel the love we felt there again here. Only when we feel the love of God and fill our hearts with it can we be truly happy.

The love of God fills the vastness of the universe. So there is no lack of love there - only we lack the willingness to do what is necessary to be able to feel it. Jesus explained how we can do this: "[Love] the Lord your God...with all your heart, and with all your soul, with all your strength, and with all your mind, and [love] your neighbor... as yourself." (Luke 10:27.)

The more we obey God, the more we desire to help others. And the more we help others, the more we love God, and it goes on and on. Conversely, the less we obey God and the more selfish we are, the less love we will feel.

Trying to find everlasting love without obeying God is like trying to quench your thirst by drinking from an empty glass—you can put it in your mouth, but the thirst remains. Similarly, trying to find love without helping and making sacrifices for others is like trying to go without food—it's against the laws of nature and bound to fail. You can't fake true love. It has to become part of our being. The prophet Mormon wrote:

"Charity is the pure love of Christ, and it endures forever; and whoever is found possessing it on the last day, it shall be well with him.

Therefore, my beloved brethren, pray unto the Father with all the strength of your heart that you may be filled with that love".

God wants so badly to help us feel His love wherever we are. I would like to give an example of this.

As a young missionary, I was sent to a small island of 700 people in a far corner of the South Pacific. I found the heat oppressive, the mosquitoes were a nuisance, the mud was everywhere, the language was impossible, and the food – well, different.

After a few months, our island was hit by a devastating hurricane. He left a trail of devastation in his wake. Crops were ruined, there were casualties, the shelter had been swept away by the wind, and the telegraph—our only link to the outside world—was destroyed. Usually, the authorities sent a boat to the island every month or two, so we timed the groceries to last four or five weeks and hoped a boat would arrive by then. But none came, and we grew weaker every day. We experienced many good deeds, but as the sixth and seventh weeks passed with hardly anything to eat, our strength dwindled noticeably. My companion, Feki, a local, helped me as best he could, but by the eighth week, I had no strength.

When the ninth week began, there was hardly any change in me on the outside. But my inner life had changed a lot. I felt the Lord's love more than ever, and I saw for myself that the love of God is "the most desirable of all things . . . yea and the greatest joy of the soul".

I was almost skin and bones now. I remember watching in awe as my heart pounded, my lungs filled with breath, and I thought what a marvel is the body that the Lord fashioned as a dwelling place for our spirits, which are marvelous as well! The thought of the enduring union of the two made possible through the love of Jesus, the atonement, and the resurrection was so inspiring and fulfilling that all health inconveniences were forgotten.

When we understand who God is, who we are, how much he loves us, and what his plan is for us, all fear will vanish. When we glimpse even a glimpse of these truths, our worldly concerns recede into the background. The thought that we actually fall for Satan's lie --- that power, fame, and fortune matter is really ridiculous—or at least would be if it weren't so sad.

I understood that, like a rocket, we must first overcome gravity in order to go into space; we must first overcome the pull of the world in order to be able to advance into the eternal spheres of knowledge and love. I realized that my life on earth could end here, but I was very calm. I knew life would go on, and it didn't matter if it was here or there. What mattered was how much love I carried in my heart. I knew I needed more of it. I knew that our joy, now and forever, is inseparable from our ability to love.

While these thoughts were still filling and uplifting my soul, a few exciting voices gradually got through to me. My associate, Loki's eyes, shone with delight as he said, "John, a boat has arrived. It's full of food. We are saved! Aren't you rejoicing?" I wasn't exactly sure, but the boat's arrival was certainly God's answer, so yes, I was rejoicing. Loki handed me something to eat and said, "There, eat!" I hesitated. I looked at the food. I looked at Loki. I looked up at the sky and closed my eyes.

I had an intense feeling. I was grateful that my life here would go on as before, but there was also a bit of melancholy – the underlying feeling that it wasn't time yet as if darkness were pushing in front of the colors of a beautiful sunset and you were becoming clear that you have to wait for another evening to experience something like this again.

I wasn't sure if I wanted to open my eyes, but when I did, I realized that God's love had changed everything. The heat, the mud, the mosquitoes, the people, the language, the food - none of that was a problem anymore. The people who threatened me were no longer my enemies. They were my brothers and sisters. Nothing makes you happier than being filled with the love of God, and it's worth every effort.

I thanked God for this special experience and everything that reminds us of His love, for the sun, the moon, the stars, the earth, the birth of a child, and the smile of a friend. I thanked him for the scriptures, for our prayers, and for the most wonderful evidence of his love, the sacrament.

As we pay close attention to the sacrament hymn, words such as "How great is wisdom and love" or "How dearly he loved us … give thanks to him by deed" (see "How great is wisdom and love," Hymns, No 122, "There Are a Hill Far Away," Hymns, no. 117) to fill our hearts with love and gratitude. As we focus on the sacrament prayers, phrases such as "always remember him," "keep his commands," and "that his spirit may be with them" will penetrate our hearts and create an overwhelming desire to do better (cf D&C 20:77-79). Then, as we partake of the bread and water with a broken heart and a contrite spirit, I know we can feel and even hear the glorious words: "I love you. Ich Liebe Dich."

I thought I would never forget those feelings, but the attraction to the world is strong, and we tend to make mistakes. But God still loves us. The Prophet Mormon still speaking:

A few months after I regained my strength, we were caught in another violent storm, this time at sea. The waves were so high that they capsized our small boat, throwing all three of us into the raging, foaming ocean. Finding myself in the middle of the stormy sea, I was amazed, scared, and a little angry. "Why is this happening?" I thought. "I am a missionary. Why am I not protected? Missionaries are not supposed to swim."

But I had to swim if I wanted to survive. Every time I complained, I went under. So it wasn't long before I stopped doing it. It is what it is, and there is no point in complaining. It took all my strength to keep my head above water and make it to shore. I had earned the Eagle Scout award, so I was a pretty good swimmer, but after a while, the wind and waves began to sap my strength. I tried again and again, but eventually, my muscles wouldn't work.

I prayed in my heart, but still, I went under. As I was about to sink into what could have been the end, the Lord filled my mind and heart with a deep love for a very special woman. It was like I could see and hear them. She may have been 13,000 kilometers from me, but the power of love spanned that distance, penetrating space and time, reaching down to me - and saving me from the depths of darkness, despair, and death, and pulling me up back to light, life, and hope. Suddenly I received a rush of renewed strength and made it to shore, where I found my comrades. Never underestimate the power of true love, for it knows no bounds.

When we are filled with the love of God, we can do, see, and understand things that we otherwise could not do, see, or understand. Filled with His love, we can endure pain, conquer fear, forgive freely, avoid arguments, find new strength, and do good and help others in ways that surprise even us.

Jesus Christ was filled with immeasurable love as He endured our pain, cruelty, and injustice beyond understanding. Because of his love for us, he overcame hurdles that would otherwise have been insurmountable. His love knows no bounds. He asks us to follow him and feel his boundless love so that we, too, can rise above the pain, cruelty, and injustice of this world and help, forgive, and be blessed.

I know he's alive; I know he loves us. I know we can feel His love here and now. I know that his voice is of perfect gentleness and penetrates deep into our souls. I know he is smiling and filled with compassion and love. I know that he is gentle, kind, and merciful and has the desire to help. I love him with all my heart. I testify that when we are ready, His pure love instantly penetrates space and time, reaching down and saving us from the depths of every raging sea of darkness, sin, sorrow, death, or despair in which we may find ourselves, and draws us up to the light and life and love of eternity. In the name of Jesus Christ. Amen."

THE LIMIT OF HIS GRACE

God's love is infinitely great. Finally, out of love for me, He sacrificed his only son so that I could be freed from guilt. And yet

His love seems to have limits. In any case, one gets the impression when reading some Bible passages that unsettle even long-standing Christians: What is the sin against the Holy Spirit that is not forgiven? If I can't forgive someone, will God not forgive me, either? Can I be lost for having once willfully sinned?

DISCOVER GOD THROUGH OTHER PEOPLE

Every human being is a unique creature of God, reflecting God's creative power and creativity. Christians who include God in their lives can use their experiences of God to help them understand God and the Bible better and to live their own relationship with God: You can pray together, read the Bible, and exchange ideas. In this way, one can meet one another in love and charity and express the lived relationship with God. It can also help your faith to read biographies of people who have experienced God now or in the past.

WHAT IS THE NATURE OF GOD'S LOVE?

Christians affirm again and again: "God is love." But is one even aware of the immense importance of this statement? Doesn't it make you ponder when you try to give a logical explanation about it?

Many suspect it. God's love must be infinite - but who can comprehend infinity? Therefore, this question is partly beyond the scope of thought. God's love cannot be fully fathomed. This is probably why God often uses human love, especially the relationship between man and woman, in the Bible to illustrate love.

ARE MY FEELINGS RETURNED?

One day the young man meets the young girl and feels attracted to her. It is easier to experience this attraction than to describe it. The young man will think about how he wants to woo the girl. At this stage, there is only one question for him. He wants to find an answer to this as soon as possible and before any other question: yes or no - will my feelings be reciprocated?

Advertising should be a delicate art. The moment violence takes the place of loving courtship; love dries up. This can also result in blame and suffering.

Love is essentially based on mutual understanding. Love includes absolute respect for the partner's voluntary decision. The basis is the free will of both parties.

THE PRINCIPLE REMAINS THE SAME.

Now, if human love serves as an illustration of divine love, then it is reasonable to assume that the principles behind human love are also applicable to God's love.

If God is love in the sense that we can understand, then we can also conclude that he is also waiting for his love to be returned. God is love, and therefore it is not in his nature to demand or compel love. Even trying to force love leads to the destruction of the basis of love. As true lovers, God demonstrates his love for us. Jesus - a man among men - becomes a partaker of our needs. Jesus exemplified love. He was serious, deadly serious. "Greater love has no man than to lay down his life for his brothers," he says in the Bible. By this, Jesus also meant his death on the cross. Here God's nature becomes transparent. He is fully committed to the people.

GOD'S COURTSHIP

What would have happened if God had created man without the possibility of free will choice? Everyone would have to do the will of God automatically, like a programmed robot. Could such a "puppet" really love? The answer is obvious. A puppet lacks personality. So she is not free to make her own decisions. The prerequisite for the essence of love is missing.

That brings us to the heart of the matter. God's courtship can be met with indifference, rejection, and hatred. If God wanted creatures who truly love him, then he had to create truly free personalities, free like himself. For he is love and created us to love. God's plan to create a truly loving person, a mate, included the risk of not being loved. God now has free partners who have the choice to love him of their own free will.

A LOVE THAT IS NOT BROKEN, IMPURE, OR FRACTURED

I am reminded of a story that happened a few years ago, at a family gathering, an -eight-year-old nephew William asked his eldest son Briton if he would like to play ball with him. Briton replied enthusiastically: "Sure! I'd love to!' After playing for a while, Briton slipped the ball and accidentally broke one of his grandparents' ancient flower pots.

Briton was terribly depressed. As he picked up the shards, William walked over to his cousin and patted him affectionately on the back. He said comfortingly, "Don't worry, Briton. When I broke something at Grandma's and Grandpa's, Grandma put her arm around me and said, 'its okay, William. You're only five."

To which Briton replied, "But William, I'm 23!"

The scriptures teach us much about how the Savior Jesus Christ can help us deal constructively with what is breaking in our lives, no matter our age. He can heal the broken relationship with God or with a person and also what is broken in ourselves.

THE BROKEN RELATIONSHIP WITH GOD

As the Savior was teaching in the temple, the scribes and Pharisees brought a woman to Him. We don't know her full story, only that she was "caught in the act of adultery" Cor became. Often the Scriptures give only a small part of human life, and on this basis, we are then inclined to praise it or to condemn it. However, a person's life cannot be pinned down to a single great hour or a single unfortunate low point in front of everyone's eyes. Instead, the scriptural accounts are meant to remind us that Jesus Christ was the answer then and is the answer today. He knows our entire history and knows what we are suffering from and what our abilities and weaknesses are.

Christ's answer to this precious daughter of God was: "Neither do I judge you. Go, and from now on, sin no more!" Instead of saying, "Go, and sin no more," He could have put it this way: "Go and change." The Savior encouraged them to repent—that is, their behavior, to change their manners, their self-esteem, and their heart.

Thanks to Christ, the decision "go and change" can also become "go and be healed" - after all, He is the source of healing for everything that has broken in our lives. As the great Mediator and Advocate with the Father, Christ sanctifies and restores broken relationships—especially our relationship with God.

Joseph Smith's translation shows that the woman did indeed follow the Savior's counsel and change her life: "And the woman praised God from that hour, and believed on his name." Unfortunately, we do not know her name or more details from their later history. In any case, she must have had great determination as well as humility and faith in Jesus Christ to repent and change in this way. We do know, however, that it was a woman who "believed in His name," knowing that she was not beyond the reach of his infinite and eternal sacrifice.

THE BROKEN RELATIONSHIP WITH A PERSON

In Luke chapter 15, there is a parable of a man who had two sons. The younger demanded his inheritance from his father, moved to a distant country, and squandered his fortune there with his unbridled lifestyle.

"When he had gotten through everything, there came a great famine in that land and he began to suffer.

So he went to a citizen of the country and imposed himself on him; he sent him to the field to tend the pigs.

He would have liked to satisfy his hunger with the fodder pods the pigs ate, but nobody gave him any of it.

Then he turned to himself and said: How many of my father's hired hands have bread in abundance, but I am dying of hunger here.

I want to get up and go to my father and say to him: Father, I have sinned against heaven and against you.

I am no longer worthy of being your son; make me one of your day workers!

Then he left and went to his father. The father saw him coming from afar and felt sorry for him. He ran to meet the son, threw his arms around his neck, and kissed him."

The fact that the father ran towards his son is a very strong statement, in my opinion. The offense that the son had inflicted on his father was certainly deep. And perhaps the father had been seriously embarrassed by his son's behavior.

So why hadn't the father waited for his son to apologize? Why not wait for a word of reconciliation and reconciliation before he himself shows forgiveness and love? I've thought a lot about that.

The Lord teaches us that the commandment to forgive applies to all: "I, the Lord, forgive whom I will forgive, but you are required to forgive everyone." Forgiving can take a tremendous amount of courage and humility. And sometimes we need time too. We are being asked to place our faith and trust in the Lord and to take responsibility for the state of our hearts because it reflects the value and power of our agency.

In describing the father in the parable of the prodigal son, the Savior emphasized that forgiveness is one of the noblest gifts we can give one another, and especially ourselves. It is not always easy to relieve our hearts through forgiveness, but it is possible through the helping power of Jesus Christ.

THAT WHICH IS BROKEN WITHIN OURSELVES

In Acts chapter 3, a man was "carried out paralyzed from birth. He was placed daily at the gate of the temple, which is called the Beautiful Gate; there he should beg for alms from those who went into the temple."

The lame beggar "was over forty years old" and had lived his entire life in a seemingly never-ending state of deprivation and waiting, dependent on the generosity of others.

One day, when he saw Peter and John going into the temple, he asked them for alms.

Peter and John looked at him, and Peter said: Look at us!

Then he turned to them, expecting to get something from them.

But Peter said: I have neither silver nor gold. But what I have I give you: In the name of Jesus Christ the Nazarene, get up and walk!

And he took him by the right hand and lifted him up. Immediately strength came to his feet and joints;

He jumped up, could stand, and walked around. Then he went with them into the temple, running and jumping and praising God."

We often find that like the paralyzed beggar at the temple gate, we patiently—or sometimes impatiently—"hope [and wait] in the Lord." We hope and wait to be healed physically or mentally. We hope and wait for answers that will satisfy us deep down. We hope and wait for a miracle.

Hoping and waiting in the Lord can carry us to holy places, where we will be refined, rejuvenated and come to know the Savior in a most personal way. Yet, there we may also ask ourselves, as we wait on the Lord, "O God, where art thou?" This place of spiritual perseverance requires our exercise of faith in Christ and renewed awareness of decide him. I know such places and know what it means to hope and wait like this.

I have a friend that has spent countless hours in a cancer care facility, suffering alongside many who also longed for healing. Some are still alive, and some are not. She has learned firsthand that deliverance from trials is different for each of us, so we should focus less on the nature of the deliverance and more on the Deliverer -- Himself. Our focus should always be on Jesus Christ!

Exercising faith in Christ means trusting not only in God's will but also in His timing because he knows what we need and when we need it. When we submit to the Lord's will, we end up getting far more than we wished for.

My dear friends, in everyone, there is something that is broken and needs to be patched, repaired, or healed. When we turn to the

Savior, set our hearts and minds on Him, and repent, He comes to us "with healing in His wings," lovingly puts His arm around us, and says, "Its okay. You're only 5 - or 16, 23, 48, 64, or 91. Together we can do it!"

I testify that nothing in life that is broken is beyond the healing, redeeming, and helping power of Jesus Christ. In the holy name of him who has the power to heal, which is Jesus Christ. Amen.

ON HOW TO STRIVE FOR THE LOVE OF GOD

The nature of God is not only there for man to believe in; it is there so that people love it. But many of those who believe in God are unable to discover this "mystery." People don't dare to love God, and they don't even try to love Him. They have never discovered that there is so much that is lovable about God; they have never discovered that God is the God who loves man and that He is the God to be loved by a man. The loveliness of God is expressed in His work: Only by experiencing His work can people discover His loveliness; only in their actual experiences can they appreciate the loveliness of God and without observing it in real life, no one can discover God's loveliness. There is so much in God that one can love, but unless they really get involved with Him, people cannot discover Him. That is, if God had not become flesh, men would not be able to deal with Him, and if they were not able to deal with Him, they would not be able to experience His work either - and so would be their Love of God fraught with much falsehood and imagination. Love for God in heaven is not as real as love for God on earth because people's knowledge of God in heaven is based on their imaginations rather than what they see with their own eyes and what they have personally experienced. When God came to earth, people were able to behold His actual deeds and His loveliness, and they could see all of His practical and normal disposition, all of which is a thousand times more real than knowledge of the God in Heaven. No matter how much people love God in Heaven, there is nothing real about that love, and it is full of human ideas. No matter how small their love for the God on earth is, that love is real; even if there is little of it, it is still real. God causes men to know Him through true work, and through this knowledge, He gains their love. It is like Peter: if he had not lived with Jesus, it would not have been possible for him to worship Jesus. So, too, was his faithfulness to Jesus built upon his association with Jesus? To make a man love Him. Remember, O LORD, your great mercy and love, for they are from of old. Remember not the sins of my youth and my rebellious ways; according to your love remember me, for you are good, O LORD. Good and upright is the LORD; therefore He instructs sinners in His ways (psalm 25).

"Love," as it is called, refers to a feeling that is pure and immaculate, where you use your heart to love, to feel, and to be considerate. In love, there are no conditions, no obstacles, and no distance. In love, there is no suspicion, no deceit, and no betrayal. In love, there is no bargain and nothing impure. When you love, you will not cheat, complain, betray, rebel, demand, or seek to get anything or get a certain amount. If you love, you will gladly make sacrifices and endure adversity, and you will become compatible with me. You will give up your everything for me; give up your family, your future, your youth, and your marriage. Otherwise, your love would not be love at all, but rather deceit and betrayal! What kind of love is yours? Is it true love? Or wrong? How much did you give up? How much did you sacrifice? How much love have I received from you? Do you know it? Your hearts are filled with evil, betrayal, and deceit, and since this is so, how many impurities are there in your love? You think you have already given up enough for me; you think that your love for me is already enough. Why, then, do your words and actions always carry rebelliousness and deceit? You follow me, but you do not recognize my word. Does that count as love? You follow me, yet you then cast me aside. Does that count as love? You follow me, but you are suspicious of me. Does that count as love? You follow me, but you cannot accept my existence. Does that count as love? You follow me, but you don't treat me as befits who I am and you make things difficult for me at every turn. Does that count as love? You follow me, yet you try to fool me and deceive me in every matter. Does that count as love? You serve me, yet you do not fear me. Does that count as love? You oppose me in every respect and in all things. Does all this count as love? You have sacrificed much, it is true, yet you have never practiced what I ask of you. Can that count as love? Careful calculation shows that there is not the faintest breath of love for me within you. After so many years of ministry and all the many words I have provided, how much have you actually accomplished? Does all this count as love? Can that count as love? Doesn't that deserve a careful look back? Making a fool of me and deceiving me in every manner. Does that count as love? You serve me, yet you do not fear me. Does that count as love?

No lesson is deeper than the lesson of loving God, and it can be said that the lesson people learn from a life of faith is how to love God. This means that if you believe in God, you must love God. If you only believe in God but do not love Him, have not attained the knowledge of God, and have never loved God with a true love that comes from within your heart, then your belief in God is in vain; if in your faith in God, you do not love God, then you live in vain, and your whole life is the lowest of all lives. If throughout your life, you have never loved or satisfied God, then what is the purpose of your life? And what is the point of your belief in God? Isn't this a waste of effort? This means if people are to believe in and love God, there is a price to pay. Instead of trying to act a certain way outwardly, they should seek inward insight into their hearts. If you sing and dance with enthusiasm but are unable to put the truth into practice, can you be said to love God? Loving God requires seeking God's will in all things and searching deep within when anything is happening to you and trying to understand God's will and trying to discern God's will in the matter, what He desires to accomplish and how you should pay attention to His will. For example, something happens that causes you to endure hardship; at this point, you should understand what God's will is and how you should pay attention to His will. You mustn't please yourself: stand back first. Nothing is more wretched than the flesh. You must strive to please God and do your duty. With such thoughts, God will bring you special enlightenment on this matter, and your heart will also find comfort.

You all know now that man's faith in God is not only for the salvation of the soul and the good of the flesh; nor does it serve to enrich one's life by loving God, and so on. As it stands, if you love God for the welfare of the flesh and momentary enjoyment, even when your love for God is at its peak and you are asking nothing, that love you seek is still impure and unsatisfactory to God. Those who use the love of God to enrich their boring lives and fill emptiness in their hearts are those who seek a comfortable life. It's not those who really seek to love God. This kind of love is against His will; it is a pursuit of emotional pleasure. God doesn't need that kind of love. Now, what kind of love is your love? Why do you love god how much true love for God do you have now? The love of most of you is like that mentioned before. This kind of love can only cultivate the present state; it cannot attain eternal permanence or take root in man. This kind of love is that of a flower that, having bloomed and withered, bears no fruit. In other words, once you have loved God in this way and there is no one to guide you along the path ahead, you will fail. If you can only love God at the time of loving God, but after that, the disposition of your life remains unchanged, you will continue to be enveloped by the influence of darkness. You will be unable to escape and free yourself from being bound to Satan and being fooled by him. No man like this can be fully won by God; in the end, his spirit, soul, and body will still belong to Satan. This is undisputed. All who cannot be totally won by God will return to their sinful place, that is, back to Satan. They will go down to the lake burning with fire and brimstone to accept the next level of God's punishment. Those won by God are those who rebel against Satan and escape from his domain. Such people will officially be counted among the people of the Kingdom. This is how the people of the kingdom come into being. Are you ready to be that kind of person? Are you ready to be won by God? Are you ready to escape Satan's domain and return to God? Do you now belong to Satan, or are you of the people of the kingdom?

Man lives under the veil of the influence of darkness and has been held in bondage to Satan's influence, unable to escape. And man's mind, after being subjected to Satan's workings, becomes more and more corrupt. It could be said that man has always lived with his corrupt satanic disposition, unable to genuinely love God. This being so, if a man is to love God, he must shed his self-righteousness, self-importance, arrogance, vanity, and the like, all of which belong to Satan's disposition. If not, his love is an impure love, a satanic love, and one that absolutely cannot receive God's approval. Without man being made perfect, dealt with, broken, trimmed, disciplined.

When people turn their hearts to God, when their hearts are able to turn fully to Him, this is the first step in man's love of God. If you want to love God, you must first be able to turn your heart to Him. What does it mean to "turn your heart to God"? It means that whatever you desire in your heart is to love and win God. This shows that you have turned your heart completely to God. Apart from God and His words, there is little else in your heart (family, wealth, husband, wife, children, etc.). Even if that is the case, such things cannot take hold of your heart, and you do not think of your future prospects but seek only to love God. By that time, you will have turned your heart completely to God. Suppose you keep making plans for yourself in your heart, always pursuing your own advantage, and constantly thinking, "When can I ask God for a little favor? When will my family become wealthy? How can I get some nice clothes?" Living in this state shows that you have not completely turned your heart to God. If you only have God's words in your heart and you can pray to God at any time and draw close to Him as if He were very close to you as if God is within you and as if you are within Him when you are in such a state, it means that your heart is in the presence of God. If you pray to God daily and eat and drink His words, always remembering the work of the Church, and if you are considerate of God's will, using your heart to love Him sincerely and satisfy His heart, then your heart will belong to God. If your heart is occupied by many other things, then it is still occupied by Satan and has not really turned to God. When a person's heart is truly turned to God, they will feel a sincere, instinctive love for Him and be able to consider God's work. Although a person may continue to have irrational and unreasonable conditions, he takes an interest in the interests of God's house, His work, and the changing of his own disposition and his heart is in the right place. Some people keep claiming that everything they do is for the church when in fact; they are working for their own good. Such people have the wrong motive. They are dishonest and deceitful, and most things they do are for their own personal gain. These types of people are not striving for the love of God. Their heart still belongs to Satan and cannot turn to God. Therefore, God has no way of obtaining these kinds of people.

At every stage of the work that God accomplishes in human beings, interactions between human beings appear as if they have arisen from human agency or interference. But behind the scenes, every stage of the work and everything that happens is a wager Satan makes before God and requires that people remain steadfast in their testimony to God. Take, for example, when Job was being tested, Satan was making a bet with God behind the scenes, and what happened to Job was man's actions and man's interference. Behind every step that God takes, you are Satan's wager with God - behind it, all is a battle. For example, if you are prejudiced against your brothers and sisters, you will have words you want to say - words you feel will displease God - but if you don't say them, you will feel uneasy inside, and at that moment, a battle will begin within you: "Am I speaking or not?" This is the fight. Thus, in everything you encounter, there is a struggle, and when there is a struggle in you, God is working in you thanks to your actual cooperation and actual suffering. Eventually, you are able to push that issue aside, and the anger is naturally extinguished. This is the effect of your cooperation with God. Everything people do requires them to pay the price for their efforts. Without actual need, they cannot satisfy God, they don't even come close to being satisfied with God, and you only give empty slogans. Can these empty slogans please God? When God and Satan fight in the spirit world, how should you please God, and how should you remain steadfast in your testimony for Him? You should know that everything that happens to you is a great test and the time when God needs you to bear witness. Outwardly they may not seem like a big deal, but when these things happen, they show whether you love God or not. If you do, you will be able to stand firm in your testimony for Him, and if you have not put love for Him into practice, it shows that you are not a pillar of truth. Into practice, realize that you are without truth and without life that you are chaff! Everything that happens to people happens when God needs their steadfastness in their testimony to Him. Nothing great has happened to you right now, and you don't bear great testimony, but every detail of your everyday life relates to the testimony of God. If you can win the admiration of your brothers and sisters, your family members, and everyone around you, when one day the unbelievers come and admire everything you do and see that everything God does is wonderful, then you will have borne your testimony. Though you have no insight and your caliber is poor, through God's perfection in you, you are able to please Him and heed His will, and show others what great work He has accomplished in people of the poorest caliber. When people come to know God and become overcomers before Satan, and are faithful to God in great measure, then none has more backbone than this group of people, and this is the greatest testimony. Although you are unable to do great work, you are able to please God. Others cannot put aside their ideas, but you can; others cannot bear witness to God during their actual experiences, but you can use your actual stature and actions to reciprocate God's love and bear a mighty testimony to Him.

That alone count as actual love for God.

The more you put the truth into practice, the more truth you possess; and the more you possess God's love; the more you will be blessed of God. If you keep practicing in this way, you will gradually see God's love in you, just as Peter recognized God: Peter said that God not only had the wisdom to create heaven and earth and all that is in them but that He also has the wisdom to do real work in people. Peter said "that He was worthy of man's love not only because of His creation of heaven and earth and all things but also because of His ability to create man, to save man, to the perfect man, and to bequeath His love for man. Peter also said that there is much in Him worthy of man's love". Peter said to Jesus, "Do you not deserve the love of men for much more than the creation of heaven and earth and all things? There is more in you to love; you act and move in real life, your spirit touches me inside, you discipline me, you blame me — these things are even more worthy of people's love." When you love, if you want to see and experience God, then you must inquire and seek in real life and be willing to put your own flesh aside. You must make this determination: You must be someone with determination, able to please God in all things without being lazy or coveting the pleasures of the flesh, not living for the flesh but living for God. There may be times when you don't satisfy God. This is because you do not understand the will of God; next time, though it will take more effort, you must please Him and not please the flesh. If your experience is like this, you will have come to know God. You will see that God could create heaven and earth and all things, that He became flesh so that men could really and actually see Him and really and actually deal with Him; that He is able to walk among men; that in real life, His Spirit can make people perfect, enabling them To see His loveliness and experience

His discipline, His chastisement, and His blessings. If you always experience this way, you will be inseparable from God in real life; and when one day your relationship with God ceases to be normal, you will be able to suffer blame and be able to feel remorse. If you have a normal relationship with God, you will never want to leave God, and when one day God says He will leave you, you will be afraid and say that you would rather die than be left by God. Once you have these emotions, you will feel that you are unable to leave God, and in this way, you will have a foundation and truly enjoy the love of God.

How much do you love God today? And how much do you know about all that God has accomplished for you? These are the things you should learn. When God arrives on earth, all that He has accomplished in man and all that He has permitted a man to see is for man to love and truly know Him. This person is able to suffer for God and has managed to get this far, which is based on the one hand, on God's love, and, on the other hand, on God's salvation. More than that, it is based on the work of judgment and chastisement that God has performed on a man. If you are without the judgment, chastisement, and trials of God, and if God has not made you suffer, then, to be honest, you do not truly love God. The greater God's work in man and the greater the suffering of man, the more it is possible to show how meaningful God's work is, and the more capable that man's heart is of truly loving God. How do you learn how to love God? Without torment and refinement, without painful trials - and if all God gave to man were grace, love, and mercy - would you be able to obtain God's, true love? On the one hand, during God's trials, man recognizes his shortcomings and sees that he is insignificant, despicable, and mean, that he has nothing and is nothing; on the other hand, during His trials, God creates various situations for a man that further enable him to experience the loveliness of God. Although the pain is great and sometimes insurmountable - even reaching the level of crushing suffering at times - the person who has experienced it sees how lovely God's work is, and only on this basis is true love for God born in man. Today man sees that with the grace, love, and mercy of God alone, he is not able to know himself, much less is he able to know the essence of man. Only through the refinement and judgment of God, only during such refinement, can man see his shortcomings and know that he has nothing. Today man sees that with the grace, love, and mercy of God alone, he is not able to know himself, much less is he able to know the essence of man. Only through the refinement and judgment of God, only during such refinement, can man see his shortcomings and know that he has nothing. Consequently, man's love for God is built upon the refinement and judgment of God. And only this basis is true love for God born in man.

Today most people do not have this realization. They believe suffering is worthless. They are rejected by the world, their home life is fraught with problems, they are not loved by God, and their prospects are poor. Some people's suffering reaches an extreme where their thoughts turn to death. This is not the true love of God; such people are cowards. They have no stamina, and they are weak and powerless! God is eager for a man to love Him, but the more man loves Him, the greater man's suffering; and the more man loves Him, the greater are man's trials. If you love Him, then every kind of suffering will come upon you - and if not, then maybe everything will go smoothly for you, and everything around you will be peaceful. If you love God, you will feel that much around you is insurmountable, and because your stature is too small, you will become refined; moreover, you are unable to please God and will always feel that God's will is too lofty, that it is beyond the reach of man. Because of all this, you will be refined - because there is much weakness within you and much that cannot satisfy God's will, you will be refined from within. But you must realize that purification can only come through refinement. So you must bear witness before God during these last days. No matter how great your suffering is, you should go to the end, and even with your last breath, you must still be faithful to God and submit to God's dominion; only this is the true love of God, and only this is the strong and overwhelming testimony. When you are tempted by Satan, you should say, "My heart belongs to God, and God has already won me. I cannot please you—I must dedicate all of my being to please God." The more you please God, the more God blesses you and the greater the strength of your love for God; so too will you have faith and determination and will feel that nothing is more valuable or meaningful than a life spent in the love of God. It can be said that man must love God in order to be carefree. Though there are times when your flesh is weak, and many real troubles come upon you, in those times, you will truly trust in God, and in your spirit, you will find comfort, and you will feel the certainty that you have something to rely on. In this way, you will be able to face many situations, and so you will not complain to God because of the torment you are going through; you will want to sing, dance and pray, gather and fellowship to reflect on God, and you will feel that all people, affairs and the things around you that are organized by God are appropriate. If you don't love God, everything you look at will weigh on you. Nothing will please your eyes. In your spirit, you will not be free but depressed, your heart will always complain to God, and you will always feel that you are suffering so many torments and that this is so unfair. If you are not striving for happiness, but striving to please God and not be accused by Satan, then such striving will give you great strength to love God. Man is capable of accomplishing whatever is spoken of God. And everything he does can satisfy God - that's what it means to possess reality. Seeking God's satisfaction is using love for God to put His words into practice. Regardless of the times - even when others are without strength - there is still a heart within you that loves God that deeply longs for God, and misses God. That's real stature. Then such striving will give you great strength to love God.

During bitter refinement, man can all too easily fall under the influence of Satan – so how should you love God during such refinement? You should find your will, lay your heart before God, and devote the rest of your life to Him. No matter how God refines you, you should be able to put the truth into practice to fulfill God's will, and you should take it upon yourself to seek God and seek an exchange. The more passive you are at times like these, the more negative you will become and the easier it will be to withdraw. When there is a need for you to fulfill your function, and though you are not serving it well, do all you can and do it using nothing but your love of God. Regardless of, what others say, whether they say you did well or badly - your motivations are right, and you are not self-righteous because you are acting on God's behalf. When others misinterpret you, you are able to pray to God and say, "Oh God, I'm not asking that others tolerate me or treat me well, nor that they understand me or approve of me; I'm just asking to be able to love you in my heart, to be calm in my heart and have a clear conscience. I do not ask that others praise me or think highly of me. I aspire only to please you from the bottom of my heart. I serve my role by doing all I can, and though I'm foolish and stupid and of small caliber and blind, I know you're lovely, and I'm ready to dedicate everything I have to you." As you pray in this way, your love for God will soar, and your heart will be much lighter. This is what is meant by exercising the love of God.

How should a man love God while being refined? By making a resolve to love God, accepting His refinement: During refinement, you are tormented inside like a knife being twisted in your heart, yet you are willing to please God using your heart that loves Him, and you are not willing to give importance to your flesh. This is what is meant by exercising the love of God. You're aching, and your suffering has reached a certain point, yet you're ready to come before God and pray and say, "Oh God, I can't leave you. Although there is darkness in me, I want to please you. You know my heart, and I wanted you to invest more of your love in me." This is the practice during refinement. Using the love of God as a foundation, refinement can bring you closer to God and make you more intimate with Him. Because you believe in God, you must surrender your heart to God. If you sacrifice your heart and lay it down before God during refinement, it will be impossible for you to reject or forsake God. Along the way, your relationship with God will become closer and more normal, and your interactions with God will become more and more frequent. If you always practice this way, you will spend more time in God's light and more time under the guidance of His words. There will also be more and more changes in your attitude and your knowledge will increase day by day. When the day comes and God's trials suddenly come upon you, not only will you be able to stand by God's side, but you will also be able to bear witness to God. At that time, you will be like Job and Peter. When you have borne witness for God, you will truly love Him and will gladly lay down your life for Him, you will be God's witness, and someone loved by God. Love that has been refined is strong, not weak. No matter when or how God subjects you to His trials, you will be able not to care whether you live or die, to joyfully lay down all things for God and happily endure all things for God—thus, your love will become pure and your faith genuine. Only then will you be someone who is truly loved by God and who has been truly made perfect by God. Again I say, at that time, you will be like Job and Peter. When you have borne witness for God, you will truly love Him and will gladly lay down your life for Him, you will be God's witness, and someone loved by God. Love that has been refined is strong, not weak. No matter when or how God subjects you to His trials, you will be able not to care whether you live or die, to joyfully lay down all things for God and happily endure all things for God—thus, your love will become pure and your faith genuine. Only then will you be someone who is truly loved by God and who has been truly made perfect by God. This is because His work demands it and, moreover, because it is needed by man. Man needs to be disciplined and judged. Only then can he attain the love of God.

Today you are all completely convinced, but as soon as you experience even the slightest setback, you are in trouble. Your stature is still too small, and you must experience more chastisement and judgment of this kind in order to gain deeper knowledge. Today you have some reverence for God, you fear God, and you know that He is the true God, but you do not have a great love for Him, let alone attained pure love. Your knowledge is too superficial, and your stature is still insufficient. When you actually encounter an environment you have not yet witnessed, too little of your entry is proactive, and you have no idea how to practice. Most people are passive and inactive. They only love God secretly in their hearts but have no opportunity for practice, nor are they clear about what their goals are. Those who have been made perfect not only have normal humanity but also have truths that transcend the limits of conscience and are higher than the standards of conscience. Not only do they use their conscience to repay God's love, but they have also come to know God and seen that God is lovely and worthy of man's love, that there is so much to love about God that man simply cannot help it than to love him. The love of God for those that have been made perfect serves to fulfill their own personal aspirations. Their love is of a spontaneous nature, a love that expects nothing in return and is not a bargain. They love God for nothing more than their knowledge of Him. Such people do not care if God bestows grace on them and are content to please God alone. They do not make a deal with God nor measure their love of God by their conscience: You have given me, so I love you in return; if you don't give me, then I have nothing for you in return. Those who have been made perfect always believe: God is the Creator, and He carries out His work on us. Having this opportunity, qualifies us through our qualification to be made perfect.

Throughout his life, Peter experienced refinement hundreds of times and endured many painful trials. This refinement became the basis of his supreme love for God and became the most significant experience of his entire life. He was able to have a supreme love for God in a way because of his determination to love God. More importantly, though, it was because of the refinement and suffering he was going through. This suffering became his guide on the way to loving God and became the thing that was most unforgettable for him. When people do not undergo the pain of refinement, when they love God, their love is full of impurities and their own preferences. Such love is full of Satan's ideas and simply incapable of satisfying God's will. Making a decision to love God is not the same as truly loving God. Although everything they think of in their hearts is for the purpose of loving God and pleasing God, as if their thoughts are devoid of any human ideas, as if they are all for the sake of God, when their thoughts are brought before God, neither do such thoughts come from God praised nor blessed. Even when people have perfectly understood all truths - when they have realized them all - this cannot be counted as loving God; one cannot say that these people actually love God. Although they have understood many truths without undergoing refinement, people are unable to put these truths into practice. Only during refinement can people understand the true meaning of these truths; only then can people truly appreciate their inner meaning. At that time, if they try again, they are able to put the truths into practice appropriately and in accordance with God's will; their human ideas are fewer at this time, their human depravity diminished, and their human emotions diminished. Only at this time is their action a true manifestation of love for God. The effect of the truth of the love of God is not achieved through spoken knowledge or mental readiness, nor can it be achieved simply by understanding it. It requires people to pay the price and go through much bitterness during refinement.

Near the end of his life, after being made perfect, Peter said: "O God! If I had a few more years to live, I would wish to attain a purer and deeper love for you." As he was about to be nailed to the cross, he prayed in his heart, "Oh God? Your time has come now; the time you prepared for me has come. I must be crucified for you, I must bear this testimony for you, and I hope that my love can satisfy your requirements and that it can become purer. Today it is comforting and reassuring for me to be able to die for you and be nailed to the cross for you, for nothing pleases me more than being able to be crucified for you and satisfying your desires and be able to give myself to you, to sacrifice my life to you. Oh, God! You are so lovely. If you allowed me to live, I would be even more willing to love you.

As long as I live, I will love you. I wish to love you more deeply. You judge me and chasten me and test me because I am not righteous because I have sinned. And your just disposition becomes more apparent to me. This is a blessing to me, for I am able to love you more deeply, and I am willing to love you that way even if you don't love me. I am ready to see your just disposition, for it further empowers me to live a meaningful life. I feel my life makes more sense now, for I am being crucified for you, and it makes sense to die for you. However, I still don't feel satisfied because I know too little about you. I know that I cannot fully fulfill your wishes and have rewarded you too little. In my life, I was unable to give you my wholeness back. I'm far from that. As I look back on this moment, I feel so obliged to you, and I have only this moment to the right all my mistakes and all the love that I have not returned to you."

Man must strive to live a meaningful life and should not be content with his present circumstances. In order to live out the image of Peter, he must have the knowledge and experiences of Peter. Man must aspire to things that are higher and deeper. He must strive for a deeper, purer love of God and a life that has value and meaning. Only that is life; only then will man be exactly like Peter. You must focus on being proactive about your entry on the positive side and not humbly allow yourself to backslide on momentary comfort while ignoring deeper, more specific, and more practical truths. Your love must be practical, and you must find a way to break away from this depraved, carefree life no different from that of an animal. You must live a meaningful life, a life of value, and not fool yourself or treat your life as if it were a toy to be played with. For all who yearn to love God, there are no unattainable truths and no rights they cannot stand by. How should you live your life? How should you love God and use that love to satisfy His desires? There is no greater concern in your life. Above all, you must have such aspirations and such tenacity and not be like these spineless wimps. You must learn how to experience meaningful life and learn meaningful truths, and you should not treat yourself carelessly in this regard. Without you noticing, your life will pass you by. Will you have another chance to love God after that? Can a man love God after he dies? You must have the same aspirations and conscience as Peter. Your life must be meaningful, and you must not play games with yourself. As a human being and as a person who aspires to God, you must be able to carefully consider how you should treat your life, how you should devote yourself to God, how you should have a more meaningful belief in God, and how you, since you love God. !!after that? Can a man love God after he dies? You must have the same aspirations and conscience as Peter. Your life must be meaningful, and you must not play games with yourself. As a human being and as a person who aspires to God, you must be able to carefully consider how you should treat your life, how you should devote yourself to God, how you should have a more meaningful belief in God, and how you, since you love God, you sh Will you have another chance to love God after that? Can a man love God after he dies? You must have the same aspirations and conscience as Peter. Your life must be meaningful, and you must not play games with yourself. As a human being and as a person desiring God, you must be able to carefully consider how you should treat your life, how you should devote yourself to God, how you should have a more meaningful belief in God, and how you, since you love God, you should love Him in a way that is purer, more beautiful, and better. Your life must be meaningful, and you must not play games with yourself. As a human being and as a person who aspires to God, you must be able to carefully consider how you should treat your life, how you should devote yourself to God, how you should have a more meaningful belief in God, and how you, since you love God, you should love Him in a way that is purer, more beautiful, and better. Your life must be meaningful, and you must not play games with yourself. As a human being and as a person who aspires to God, you must be able to carefully consider how you should treat your life, how you should devote yourself to God, how you should have a more meaningful belief in God, and how you, since you love God, you should love Him in a way that is purer, more beautiful, and better.

If people want to love God, they must taste God's loveliness and see God's loveliness; only then can a heart be awakened in them that love God, a heart that is willing to faithfully expend itself for God. God does not make people love Him by word and expression or their imagination, and He does not force people to love Him. Instead, He causes them to love Him of their own free will, and He lets them see His sweetness in His work and in His utterances, after which the love of God is brought forth in them. Only in this way can people truly testify before God. People love God not because others have compelled them to, nor is it a passing emotional impulse. They love God because they have seen His loveliness; they have seen that there is so much of Him worthy of men's love because they have seen God's salvation, wisdom, and wondrous works - and therefore, they truly praise God and truly long for Him, and it was made in them aroused such passion that they could not survive without attaining God. The reason those who truly bear witness to God are able to bear overwhelming witness to Him is that their witness rests on the foundation of true knowledge and desire of God. It is not based on an emotional impulse but on knowledge of God and His disposition. Because they have come to know God, they feel that they must surely bear witness to God and cause all who long for God to get to know God and become aware of God's sweetness and genuineness. Like men's love of God, their testimony is spontaneous, genuine, and has real meaning and value. It's not passive or hollow and meaningless. The reason only those who truly love God have the greatest worth and purpose in their lives and only truly believe in God is that because they walk in God's light, these people are able to live for God's work and guidance; they do not live in darkness, but they live in the light; they do not lead meaningless lives, but lives blessed by God. Only those who love God are able to bear witness to God, and only they are God's witnesses; only they are blessed by God, and only they are able to receive God's promise. Those who love God are God's intimates, they are God's loved ones, and they can enjoy blessings with God. Only people like these will live to all eternity, and only they will live under God's care and protection forever. God is there to be loved by man, and He is worthy of the love of all men, but not all men are capable of loving God, and not all men can testify of God and hold power with God. Because they are able to bear witness to God and devote all their efforts to God's work, those who truly love God can walk anywhere under the heavens without anyone daring to oppose them, and they can rely on the exercise of power on earth and rule over all of God's people. These people have come together from all over the world, they speak different languages , and they have different skin colors, but their existence has the same meaning; they all have a heart that loves God, they all testify to the same thing, and they have the same determination and desire. Those who love God are free to roam the world; those who bear witness to God can travel throughout the universe. These people are loved by God, they are blessed by God, and they will live in His light forever. Those who love God can roam freely in the world; those who bear witness to God can travel throughout the universe. These people are loved by God, they are blessed by God, and they will live in His light forever. Those who love God can roam freely in the world; those who bear witness to God can travel throughout the universe. These people are loved by God, they are blessed by God, and they will live in His light forever.

Made in the USA
Columbia, SC
01 December 2022